Maths Revision Booklet
for CCEA GCSE 2-tier specification
M4

Neill Hamilton

Contents

You are permitted to use a calculator in this examination.

Revision Exercise 1 3

Revision Exercise 2 11

Revision Exercise 3 18

Revision Exercise 4 26

Revision Exercise 5 32

Answers 39

Dedicated to the 5 best grandchildren in the world Cadence, Lily, Willow, Quinn and Rory and the best marathon runner ever, David.

Revision Exercise 1

1. Look at the shape below. All measurements are in centimetres.

   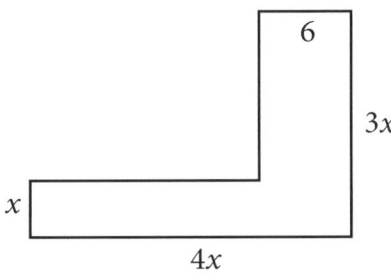

   (a) Show that its area is given by $4x^2 + 12x$

   (b) Find the value of x when the area is 40 cm²

   Answer $x = $ _____

2. (a) Find the equation of the straight line L which passes through the points (3, −4) and (1, −8).
   (**Hint: You have to learn the coordinate geometry formulae. The formulae are not given in the exam.**)

   Answer _____

   (b) Find the equation of the straight line which passes through (−2, 5) parallel to L.

   Answer _____

   (c) Find the equation of the straight line which passes through (−2, 5) perpendicular to L.

   Answer _____

3. The table below shows the heights of 240 objects to the nearest centimetre.

Height (h cm)	1–4	5–8	9–12	13–16	17–20	21–24	25–28
Frequency	10	32	44	78	40	28	8

(a) Complete the cumulative frequency table below.

Height (less than) cm	0.5	4.5	8.5	12.5	16.5	20.5	24.5	28.5
Cumulative Frequency	0	10	42					240

(b) Draw the cumulative frequency curve on the grid below.

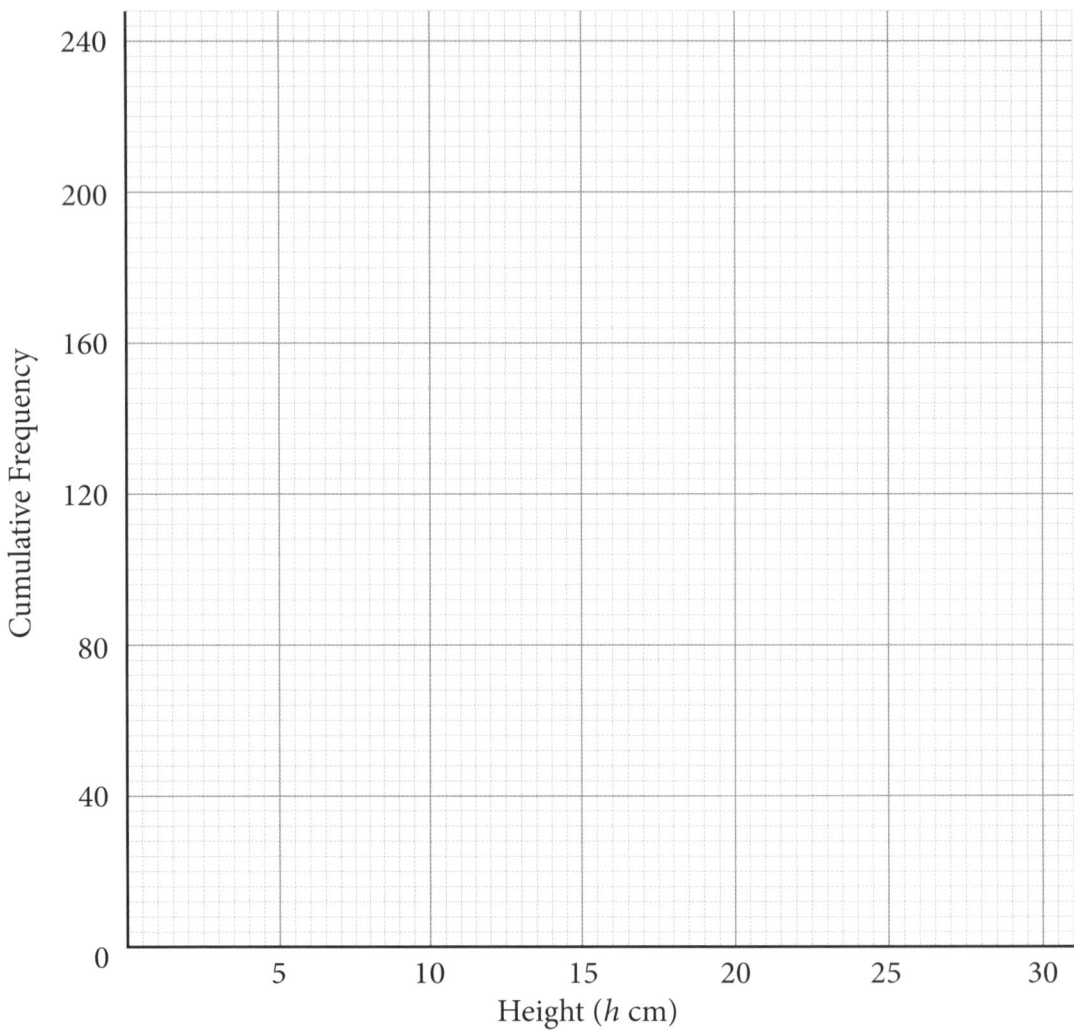

(c) Use your cumulative frequency curve to estimate:
  (i) the median,

Answer _____ cm

  (ii) the inter-quartile range,

Answer _____ cm

  (iii) how many heights are between 7 cm and 22 cm.

Answer _____

(d) The tallest 15% are discarded. Find the tallest height kept.

Answer _____ cm

(e) Draw a box plot of the heights on the grid below.

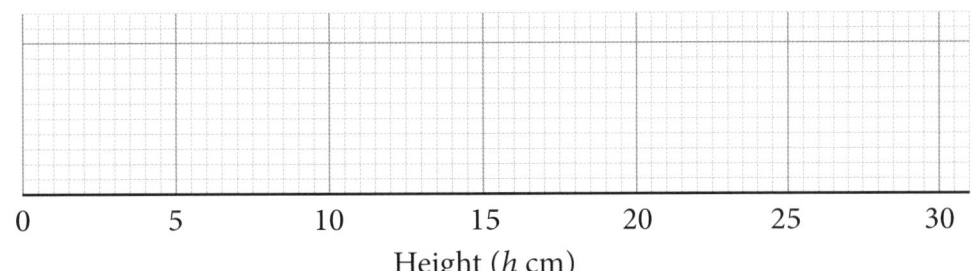

Height (h cm)

4. Factorise completely:
   (a) $8xn + 4xc - 6n - 3c$

   Answer _____

   (b) $q^2 - 3q - 40$

   Answer _____

   (c) $7(f + 3) - 4(f + 3)^2$

   Answer _____

   (d) $3t^2 - 48v^2$

   Answer _____

5. Solve:
   (a) $6h^2 + h = 0$

   Answer _____

   (b) $t^2 - 9t + 18 = 0$

   Answer _____

6. ABC is a triangle. A(2, −4), B(3, 2), C(−3, 3). Prove that ABC is a right-angled triangle.

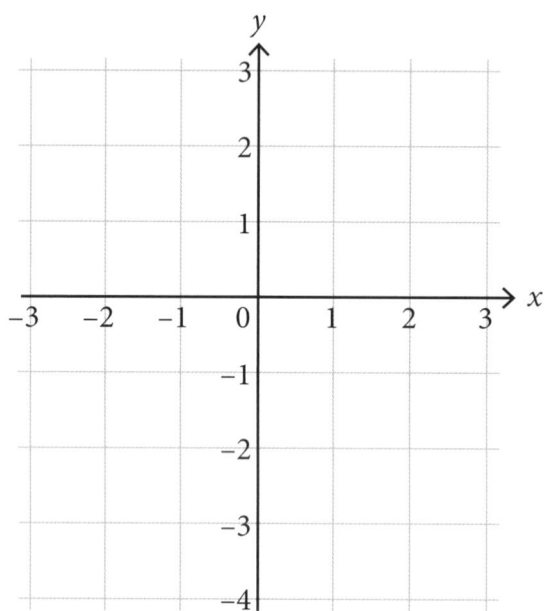

7. C is the centre of the circle shown below. PQ is parallel to SR. ∠PQS = 34°

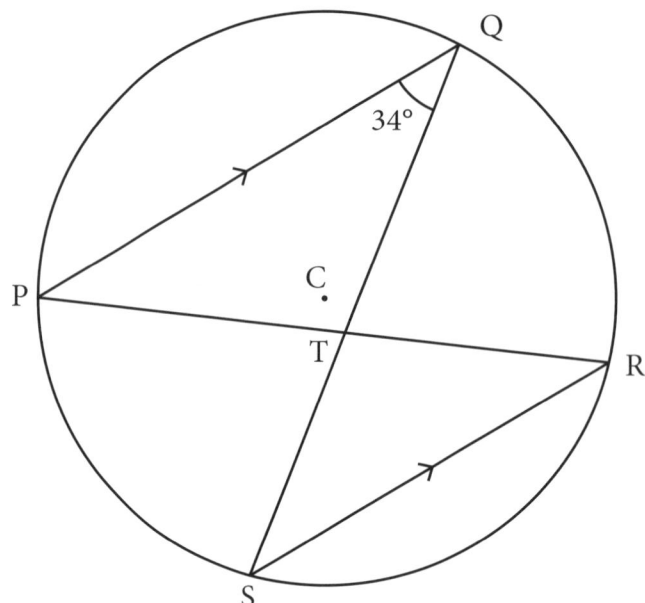

Find the size of the angle:
(a) ∠PRS

Answer _____°

(b) ∠QSR

Answer _____°

(c) ∠PTQ

Answer _____°

(d) ∠PTS

Answer _____°

8. There are 976 pupils in a school.
   A stratified sample by age is taken. Some information is given in the table below.

Age (years)	4 to 6	7 to 8	9	10 to 11
Number of pupils	272		144	
Number in sample	34	27		

Complete the table.

9. Solve the following:

(a) $\dfrac{9 - 3x}{4} = 5 - 2x$

Answer $x =$ _____

(b) $\tfrac{2}{3}(x + 1) + \tfrac{1}{4}(x - 4) = 7$

Answer $x =$ _____

(c) $\dfrac{2x - 1}{3} - \dfrac{x + 3}{4} = 1$

Answer $x =$ _____

10. Simplify:

(a) $\dfrac{m}{n} - \dfrac{n}{m}$

Answer _____

(b) $\dfrac{n}{4} + \dfrac{6}{n}$

Answer _____

(c) $3q - \dfrac{q}{4}$

Answer _____

11. The graph of $v = pm + q$ is shown below.

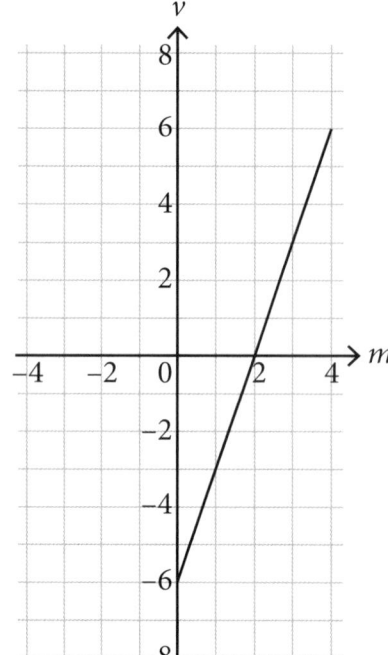

Find the value of:

(a) p

Answer $p =$ _____

(b) q

Answer $q =$ _____

Revision Exercise 1

12. Look at the shape below. All measurements are in centimetres.

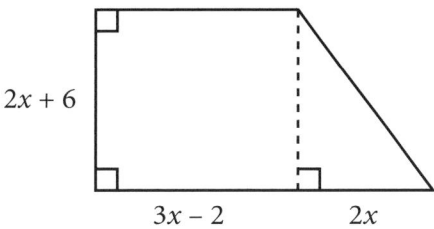

(a) Show that its area is given by $8x^2 + 20x - 12$

(b) Find the value of x when the area is 60 cm²

Answer $x =$ _____ cm

13. (a) Find the equation of the straight line L which passes through the points $(-1, 6)$ and $(2, -6)$.
(Hint: You have to learn the co-ordinate geometry formulae. They are not given in the formula booklet.)

Answer _____

(b) Find the equation of the straight line which passes through $(3, -4)$ parallel to L.

Answer _____

(c) Find the equation of the straight line which passes through $(8, -2)$ perpendicular to L.

Answer _____

14. C is the centre of the circle shown below. TA is a tangent. ∠ADB = 28°

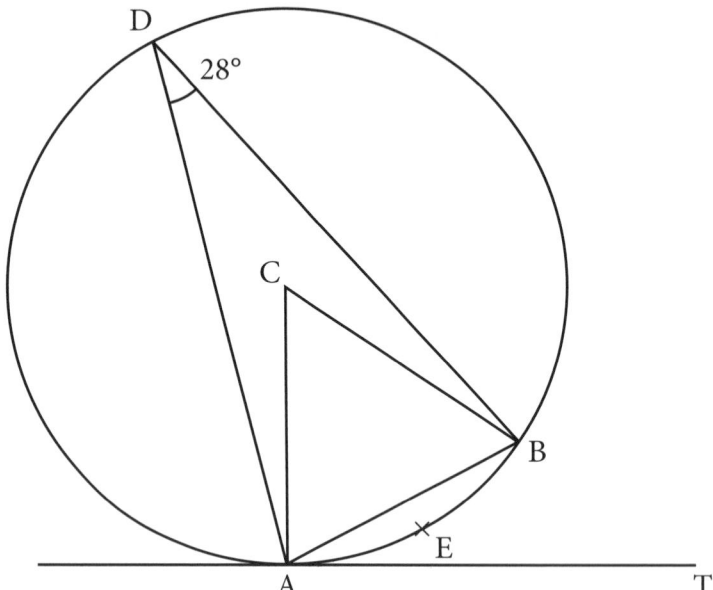

Find the sizes of the angles:
(a) ACB

Answer _____ °

(b) CAB

Answer _____ °

(c) TAB

Answer _____ °

(d) AEB

Answer _____ °

Revision Exercise 2

1. Solve:
   (a) $c^2 + 7c + 10 = 0$

   Answer $c =$ _____

   (b) $16f^2 = 49$

   Answer $f =$ _____

   (c) $w^2 + 3w - 40 = 0$

   Answer $w =$ _____

2. Solve the following.
   (Hint: You can factorise these expressions)

   (a) $8c^2 - 50 = 0$

   Answer $c =$ _____

   (b) $2d^2 - 4d - 70 = 0$

   Answer $d =$ _____

   (c) $3e^2 - 2e - 8 = 0$

   Answer $e =$ _____

   (d) $6f^2 + 19f + 10 = 0$

   Answer $f =$ _____

   (e) $5g^2 - 30g + 40 = 0$

   Answer $g =$ _____

3. The lengths of different objects are given below correct to the nearest centimetre.

Length (*l* cm)	1–5	6–15	16–17	18–22	23–37	38–39
Frequency	190	270	68	110	210	52

Draw a histogram on the grid below to illustrate this data.
(Hint: You must show all your working)

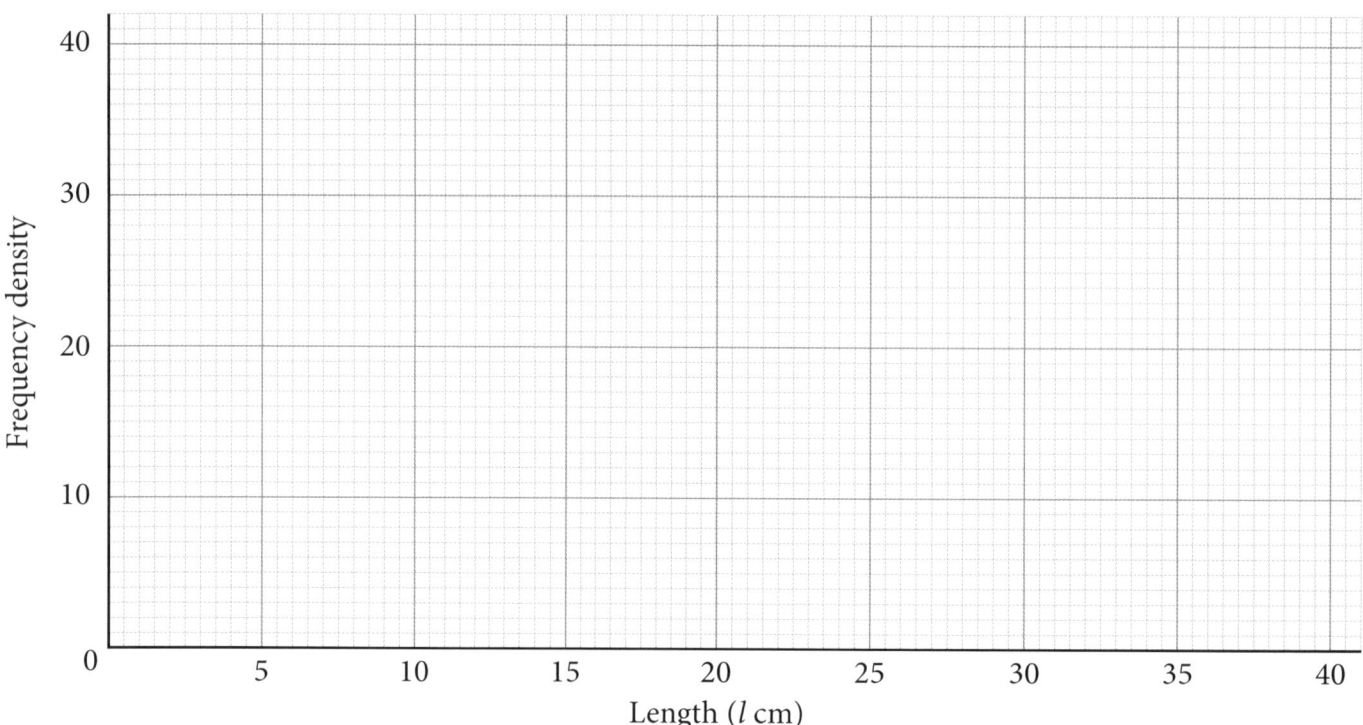

4. Expand and simplify:

   (a) $(4x + 3y)(2x - 7y)$

   Answer _____

   (b) $(5a - 6b)^2$

   Answer _____

   (c) $(3k - 2m)(k + 4m) - (2k + 3m)^2$

   Answer _____

Revision Exercise 2

5. (a) Write down the equation of the straight line shown below.

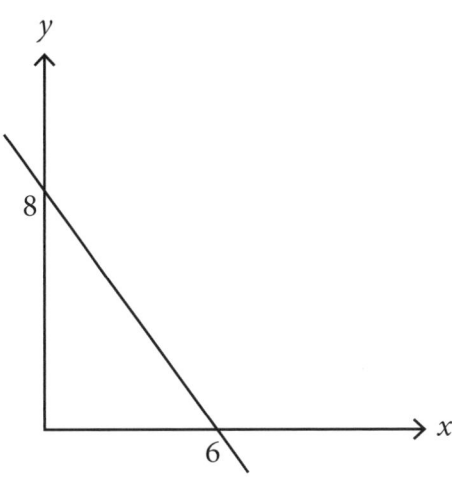

Answer _____

(b) Write down the gradient of the straight line perpendicular to the straight line drawn.

Answer _____

6. Solve:

(a) $\dfrac{12}{x} + \dfrac{6}{x-3} = 4$

Answer $x =$ _____

(b) $\dfrac{8}{x} - \dfrac{3}{x+1} = 3$

Answer $x =$ _____

7. O is the centre of the circle. AE is a tangent and ∠EAB = 35° and ∠ABC = 52°

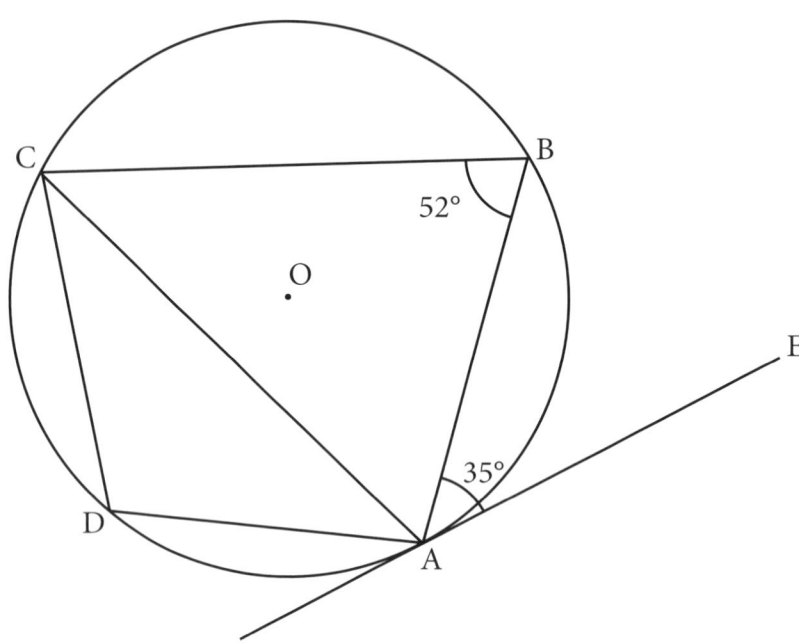

(a) Explain why ∠ACB = 35°

Answer _____

_____

(b) Explain why ∠CDA = 128°

Answer _____

_____

(c) Explain why ∠OAE = 90°

Answer _____

_____

(d) Work out the size of ∠COA

Answer _____

8. The histogram shown below represents the lengths, in centimetres, of objects in a box.

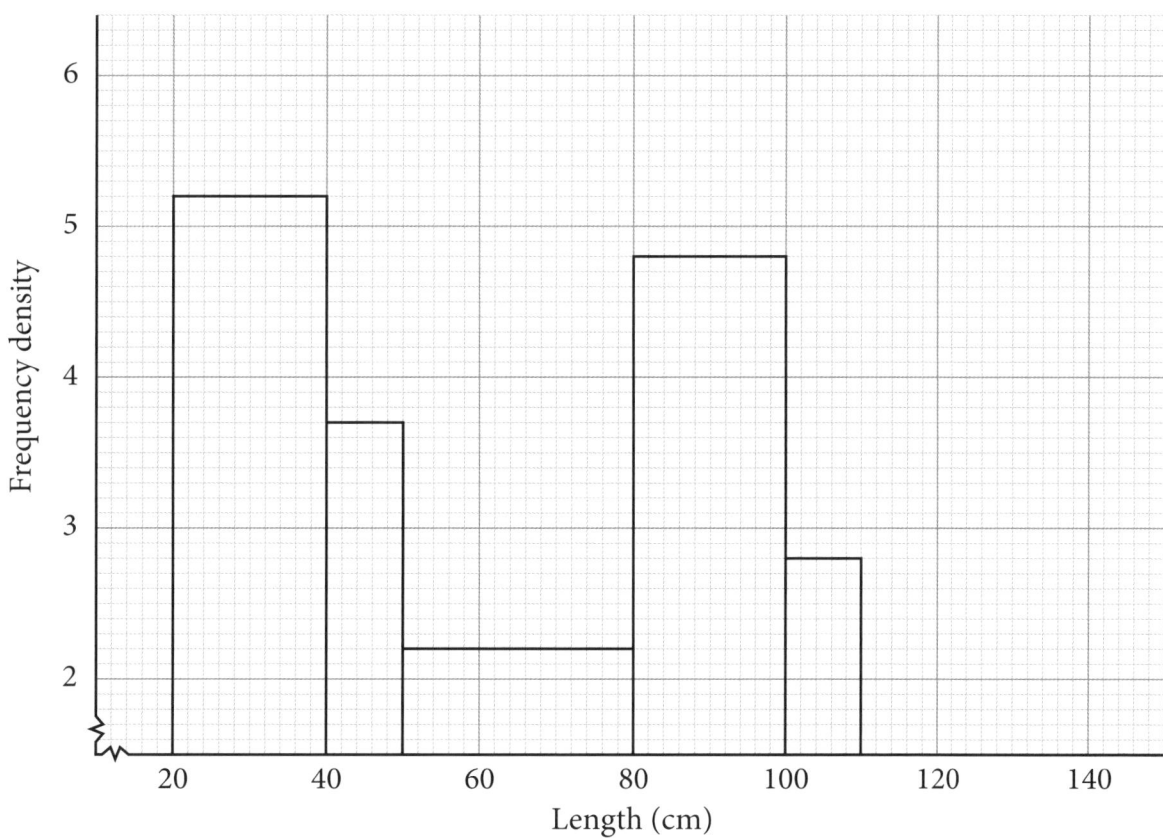

(a) Work out the total number of objects in the box.

Answer _____ objects

(b) There are 102 objects in another box. Their lengths, l cm, are such that $110 < l \leq 140$
Add this information to the histogram.

9. Find the equation of the straight line which is:

(a) parallel to the straight line $y = 4x + 3$ and which passes through $(0, 2)$,

Answer _____

(b) perpendicular to the straight line $y = 2x - 5$ and which passes through $(3, 1)$.

Answer _____

10. Solve the equation:

$$\frac{5}{2x-1} - \frac{4}{2-x} = 5$$

Answer $x =$ _____

11. (a) Find ∠BAC in the diagram below.
    (**Hint: Give your answer correct to 1 decimal place. Make sure your calculator is in degree mode.**)

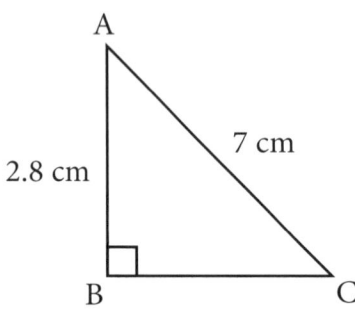

Answer _____ °

(b) Find EF in the diagram below.

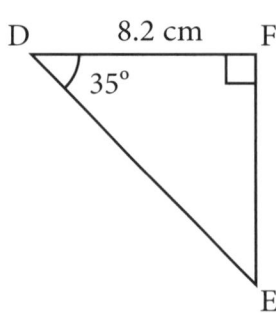

Answer _____ cm

12. A pen is measured as 14.7 cm long, correct to 1 decimal place.
    Find the least and greatest total length of 7 of these pens.

Least _____ cm

Greatest _____ cm

13. Brenda deposits £P in an ISA account which pays x% compound interest each year.
After 1 year the total value of her deposit is £5824. After 2 years the total value of her deposit is £6056.96
Find:
(a) the value of x,

Answer x = _____

(b) the value of P,

Answer P = _____

(c) the total value of her deposit after 3 years.

Answer £ _____

14. PQRS, shown below, is a trapezium where PS = 9.4 cm, SR = 5.8 cm and ∠PSR = 130°
Calculate:
(a) QR
(b) PQ
(Hint: Draw out a right-angled triangle.)

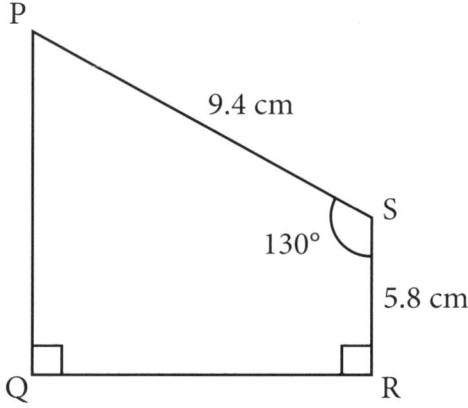

Answer (a) _____ cm

Answer (b) _____ cm

Revision Exercise 3

1. TP is a vertical pole. AP = 1.26 m and AB = 1.8 m.
   The angle of elevation of T from A is 28°

   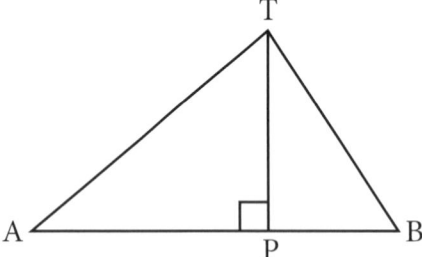

   Calculate:
   (a) TP

   Answer _____ m

   (b) the angle of elevation of T from B.

   Answer _____ °

2. The base radius and height of a cylindrical container were measured as 3.24 cm and 6.93 cm, each correct to the nearest one hundredth of a centimetre.

   (a) 30 of these containers are stacked each on top of each other.
   Calculate the maximum possible height.

   Answer _____ cm

   (b) 12 of these containers are placed side by side in a box.
   Calculate the minimum possible width of the box.

   Answer _____ cm

3. From a point X on top of a cliff XY the angle of depression of a boat at Z is 32° as shown below. YZ = 24 m.

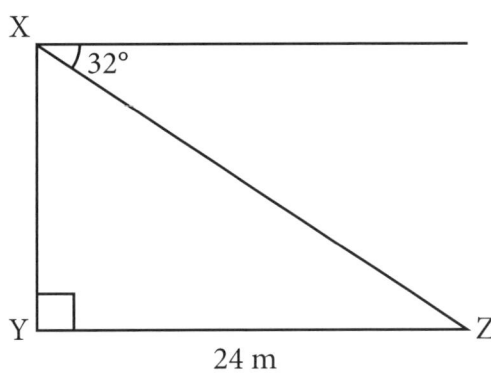

Calculate
(a) XY

Answer _____ m

(b) XZ

Answer _____ m

4. The base area and height of a cuboid were measured as 56 cm² to the nearest cm², and 8.7 cm to the nearest one tenth of a centimetre.

(a) Calculate the maximum possible volume of the cuboid.

Answer _____ cm³

The length of this cuboid was measured as 12 cm correct to the nearest centimetre.

(b) Calculate the minimum possible breadth of the cuboid.

Answer _____ cm

5. The table below gives values of *v* and *T*.

v	1	1.41	1.73	2	2.24	2.45
T	7.6	8.2	8.8	9.4	10	10.6

(a) Complete the following table giving values to the nearest integer where appropriate.

v^2	1	2				
T	7.6	8.2	8.8	9.4	10	10.6

(b) By drawing a graph on the grid below, show that the relationship between *v* and *T* can be expressed as $T = av^2 + b$

(Hint: You must explain why the equation has this form.)

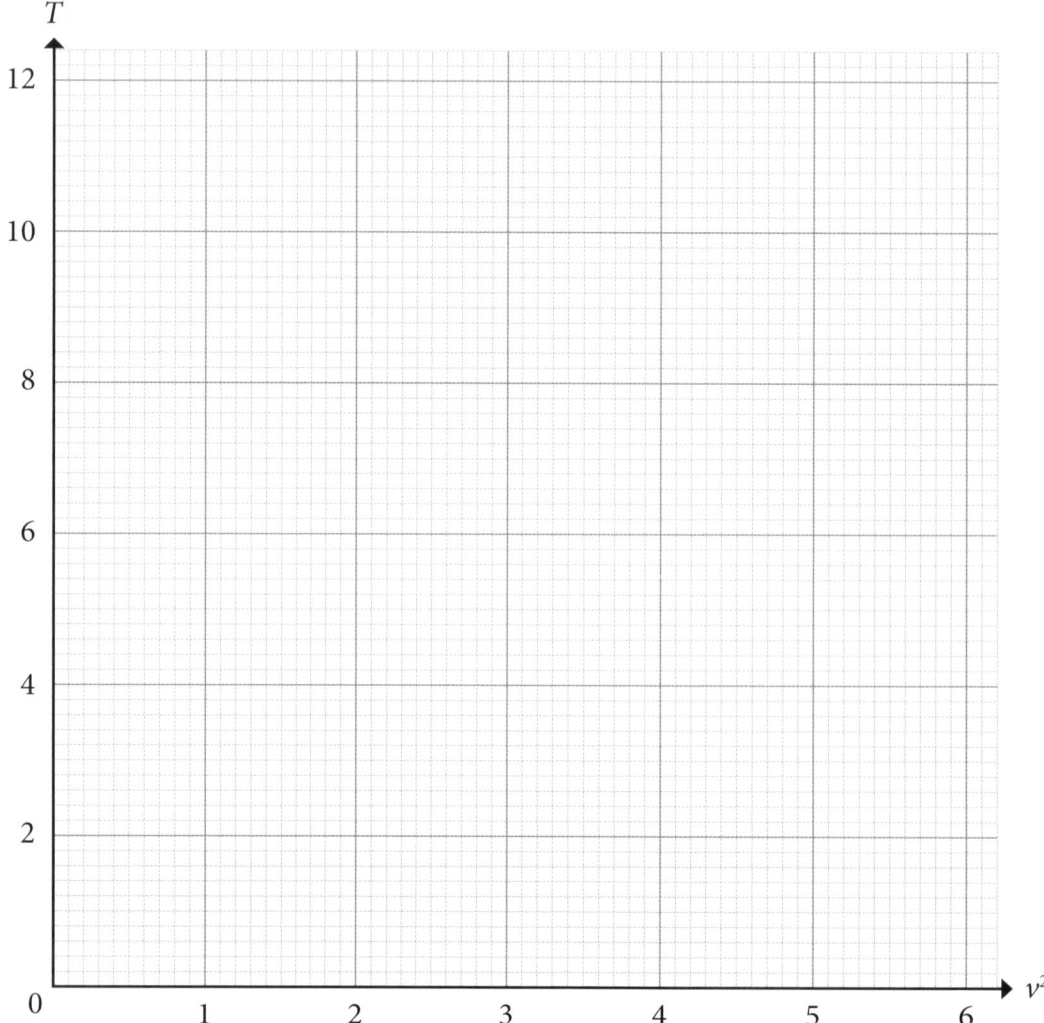

Answer _____

(c) Hence determine the values of **(i)** *a* **(ii)** *b*

Answer **(i)** $\qquad\qquad\qquad\qquad\qquad\qquad\qquad\qquad\qquad\qquad\qquad\qquad$ a = _____

Answer **(ii)** $\qquad\qquad\qquad\qquad\qquad\qquad\qquad\qquad\qquad\qquad\qquad\qquad$ b = _____

Revision Exercise 3

6. In the diagram below BC = 9.6 cm, ∠ADB = 42° and ∠CBD = 54°
   Calculate AB.
   (Hint: Start with the triangle in which you know 2 quantities as well as the right angle)

   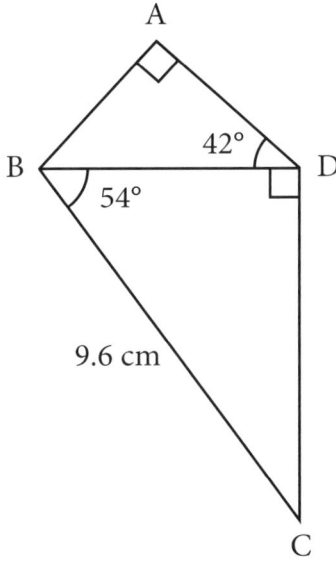

   Answer _____ cm

7. Solve the following equations giving your answers to 3 decimal places.
   (Hint: The equations must not factorise since you are told to round your answers. You must use the formula from the formula booklet.)

   (a) $4x^2 - 7x - 8 = 0$

   Answer $x =$ _____

   (b) $6x(x + 4) = 5$

   Answer $x =$ _____

8. Solve the equation:

   $\dfrac{2 - x}{2} - \dfrac{4x - 3}{3} = 13$

   Answer $x =$ _____

9. (a) Show that the equation $\dfrac{18}{x} + \dfrac{15}{x-3} = 8$ can be rearranged into the form $8x^2 - 57x + 54 = 0$

(Hint: You must show all your work. Start with the original equation and try to end up with the second equation)

(b) Hence solve $\dfrac{18}{x} + \dfrac{15}{x-3} = 8$

(Hint: Solve the quadratic equation to find x)

Answer $x =$ _____

10. Values a, b and c are recorded as 8.4, 7.9 and 5.3 each correct to one decimal place. Calculate the:

(a) lower bound of c^2

Answer _____

(b) upper bound of $\dfrac{a}{b}$ to 2 decimal places

Answer _____

(c) lower bound of $b - c$

Answer _____

11. C is the centre of the circle shown below. TA and TB are tangents drawn from T.
∠TAB = 58°

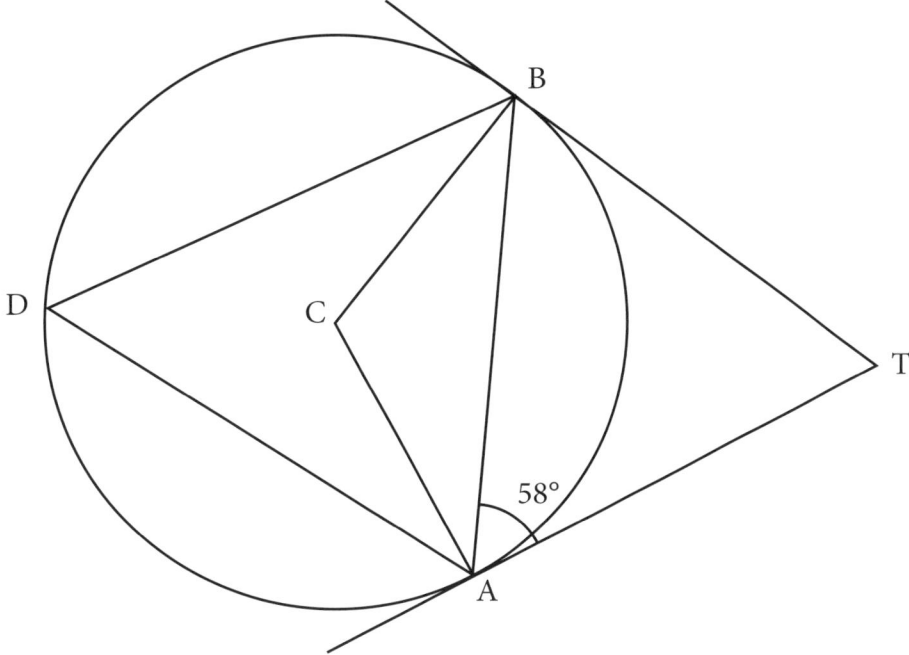

Find the sizes of the angles:

(a) ∠ADB

Answer _____ °

(b) ∠ACB

Answer _____ °

(c) ∠CAB

Answer _____ °

(d) ∠ATB

Answer _____ °

12. A car depreciates by 18% per year. It originally cost £9600. After how many years will its value have halved?

Answer _____ years

13. (a) (i) Factorise $3a^2 + 6a$

    Answer _____

   (ii) Hence simplify:
   (**Hint: 'Hence' means you should use your previous answer**)

   $$\frac{3a^2 + 6a}{a^2 - 4}$$

    Answer _____

(b) (i) Factorise $x^2 - 2x - 3$

    Answer _____

   (ii) Hence simplify:

   $$\frac{x^2 - 2x - 3}{x^2 - 5x + 6}$$

    Answer _____

(c) (i) Factorise $t^2 + 11t + 28$

    Answer _____

   (ii) Hence simplify:

   $$\frac{t^2 + 11t + 28}{t^2 + 5t - 14}$$

    Answer _____

14. The histogram below shows the heights, in cm, of different objects.

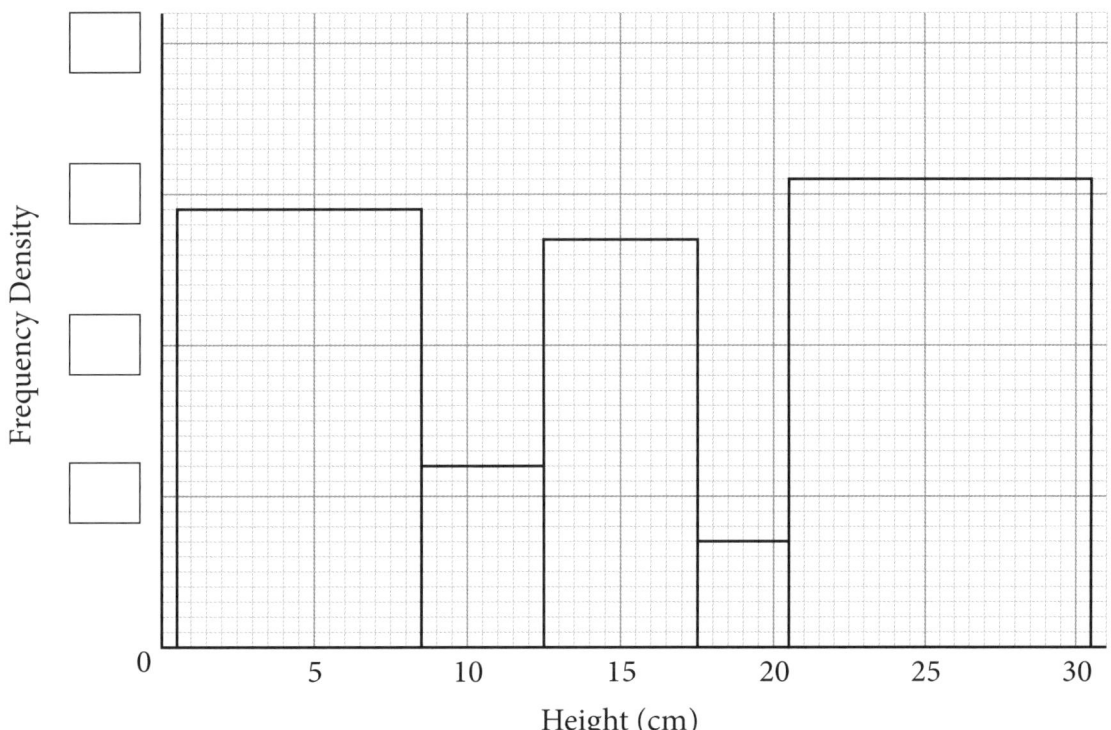

768 objects have heights between 1 and 8 cm, measured to the nearest cm.

(a) Write down the scale of the vertical axis.

Answer 1 cm = _____

(b) Complete the vertical axis by writing the correct numbers in the boxes.

(c) Hence complete the table below.

Height (cm)	Frequency
1–8	768

Revision Exercise 4

1. Simplify the following.
   (Hint: **Factorise the numerator and the denominator. Do not try to simplify your answer further than it will simplify.**)

   (a) $\dfrac{x^2 - 2x - 15}{x^2 - 9}$

   Answer _____

   (b) $\dfrac{x^2 - 10x + 21}{x^2 - x - 6}$

   Answer _____

   (c) $\dfrac{2x^2 + x - 6}{6x^2 - 11x + 3}$

   Answer _____

   (d) $\dfrac{16x^2 - 1}{12x^2 + 3x}$

   Answer _____

   (e) $\dfrac{x^2 - x - 2}{x^2 - 7x + 10}$

   Answer _____

   (f) $\dfrac{x^2 + 7x + 12}{x^2 + 2x - 8}$

   Answer _____

2. The rectangle and square below both have the same area.

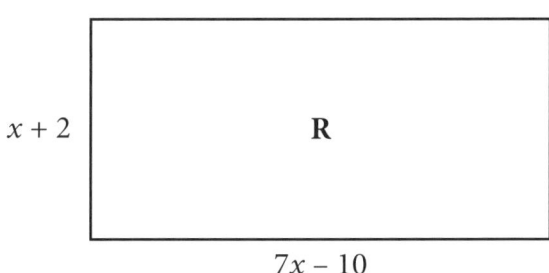

(a) Prove that $x^2 - 8x + 12 = 0$

(b) Hence find 2 possible values for x.

Answer $x =$ _____ or _____

3. Solve the following:

(a) $\dfrac{4}{x+5} + \dfrac{1}{x+2} = 1$

Answer $x =$ _____

(b) $\dfrac{10}{x+1} - \dfrac{2}{x-2} = 1$

Answer $x =$ _____

4. A metal plate is in the shape of a sector AOB of a circle of radius 6 cm and angle AOB = 30°
   The force acting on this plate is 56 N.
   Find the pressure on the plate.

   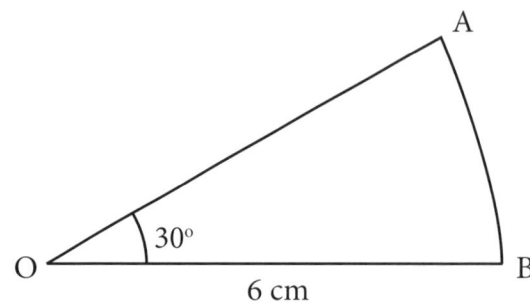

   Answer _____

5. The scores of 10 cricketers in an innings were:

   9   14   4   30   27   24   32   26   5   19

   Find the
   (a) median,

   Answer _____

   (b) lower quartile,

   Answer _____

   (c) upper quartile,

   Answer _____

   (d) interquartile range.

   Answer _____

6. There are 456 men, 342 women and 513 children on a package holiday.
   The tour operator wants to take a stratified sample of size 69 of men, women and children.
   How many men will be included in this sample?

   Answer _____ men

Revision Exercise 4

7. The values A, B, C and D are measured as 8.4, 9.7, 5.3 and 1.7 each, correct to 2 significant figures. Work out:
   (a) the greatest possible value of A + D,

   Answer _____

   (b) the least possible value of A(B − C).

   Answer _____

8. The length and breadth of a rectangle are measured as 7.4 cm and 6.8 cm each correct to 1 decimal place. Work out the greatest possible length of the diagonal.

   Answer _____

9. AOB is a quarter of a circle centre O radius 6 cm as shown below.

   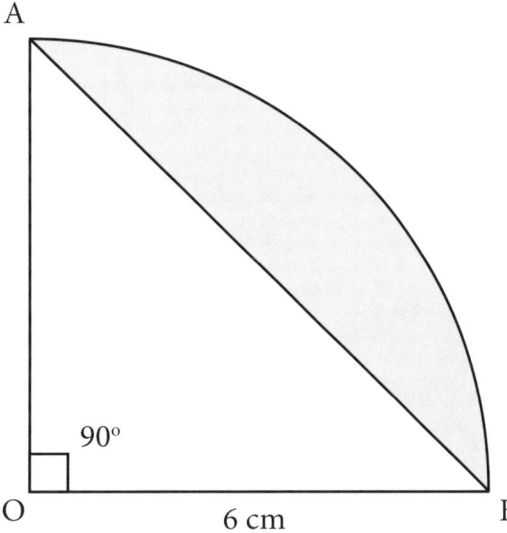

   Work out:
   (a) the area of the shaded segment,

   Answer _____

   (b) perimeter of the shaded segment.

   Answer _____

10. The length and breadth of a rectangular sheet of plastic are measured as 8.4 cm and 3.2 cm each correct to 1 decimal place. A circle of radius 1.4 cm correct to 1 decimal place is cut out of the plastic.
Work out the greatest possible area left.

Answer _____

11. PQR is a right angled triangle in which angle Q = 90°. PR = 16 cm and QR = 12 cm, each measured correct to the nearest integer. Work out:
(a) the maximum value of PQ,

Answer _____

(b) the minimum value of angle QRP.

Answer _____

12. Simplify:

(a) $\dfrac{4}{x-3} + \dfrac{2}{2x+1}$

Answer _____

(b) $\dfrac{5}{3x-2} - \dfrac{2}{x+5}$

Answer _____

Revision Exercise 4

13. A car travels 20 km at an average speed of $(x + 3)$ km/h.
It travels 36 km at an average speed of $(2x - 1)$ km/h.
Find the total time taken.

Answer _____

14. There are 52 pupils in Year 12.

4 study Art, Biology and Child Development.
9 study Art and Biology.
6 study Art and Child Development.
10 study Biology and Child Development.
18 study Art.
24 study Biology.
20 study Child Development.

(a) Show this information on a Venn diagram.

(b) Hence find how many study none of these subjects.

Answer _____

Revision Exercise 5

1. A test tube consists of an open cylinder attached to a hemisphere as shown below. The base radius and height of the cylinder are 3 cm and 12 cm.

   Work out:
   (a) the total volume of the test tube,

   Answer _____

   (b) the total surface area of the test tube.

   Answer _____

2. The base radius of the frustum of a cone is 6 cm and the top radius of the frustum is 1.5 cm as shown below. The slanted height makes 75° with the base.

   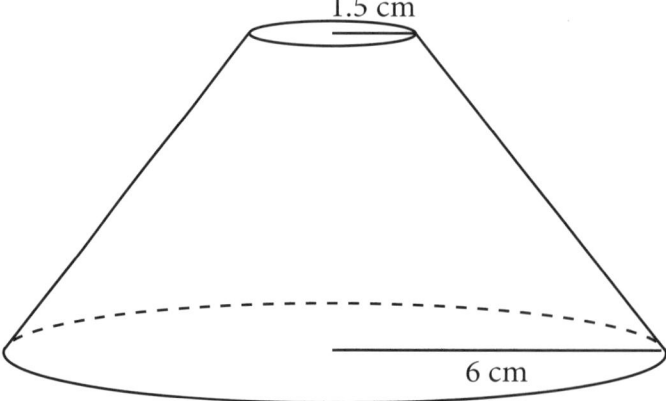

   Work out the volume of the frustum.

   Answer _____

3. The base radius of the frustum of a cone is 4 cm and the top radius of the frustum is 1.2 cm as shown. The slant height of the frustum is 16 cm. The slant height of the original cone is 22.86 cm.

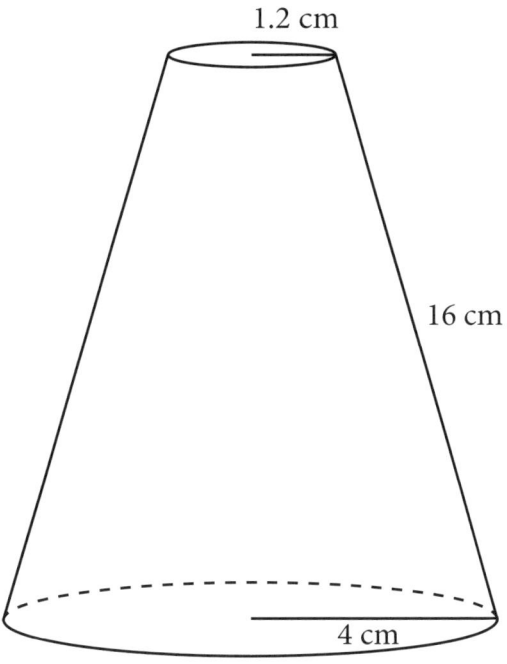

Work out the volume of the frustum. Give your answer to the nearest integer.

Answer _____

4. The base radius of the frustum of a cone is 2.4 cm. The height of the original cone is 14.4 cm. The height of the cone which is cut off is 4.8 cm. The radius of the top of the frustum is 0.8 cm.

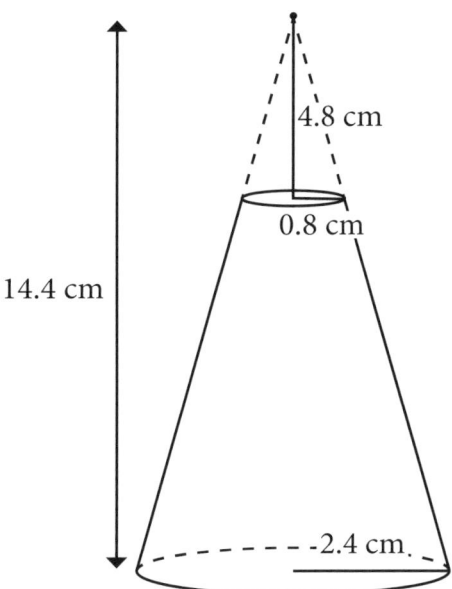

Work out the curved surface area of the frustum. Give your answer to the nearest integer.

Answer _____

5. There are 77 people in a gym.

   x join the Body Pump class, the Spinning class and the Infinity class.
   9 join the Body Pump class and the Spinning class.
   13 join the Body Pump class and the Infinity class.
   14 join the Spinning class and the Infinity class.
   29 join the Body Pump class.
   36 join the Spinning class.
   37 join the Infinity class.
   6 join none of these classes.

   (a) Show this information on a Venn diagram.

   Hence find:
   (b) the value of x, i.e. how many joined all three classes.

   Answer _____

   (c) how many joined only two of these classes.

   Answer _____

6. The histogram below shows the weights of different objects.

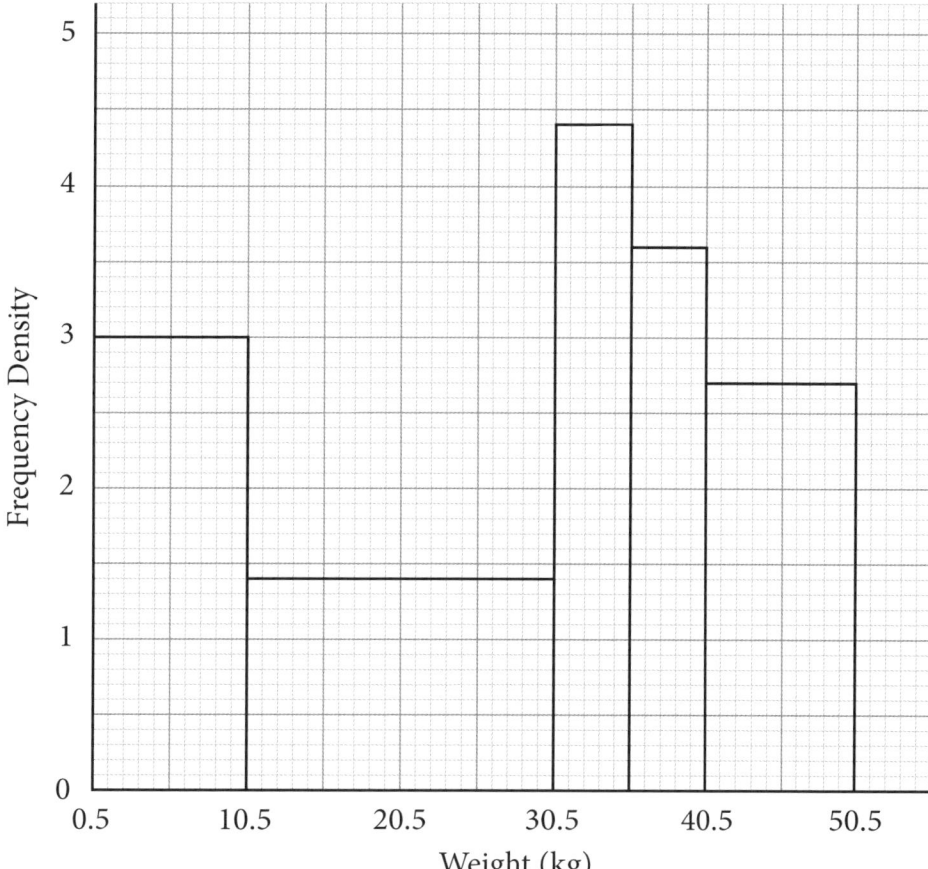

Work out the mean weight.

Answer _____

7. The histogram below shows the lengths of different objects.

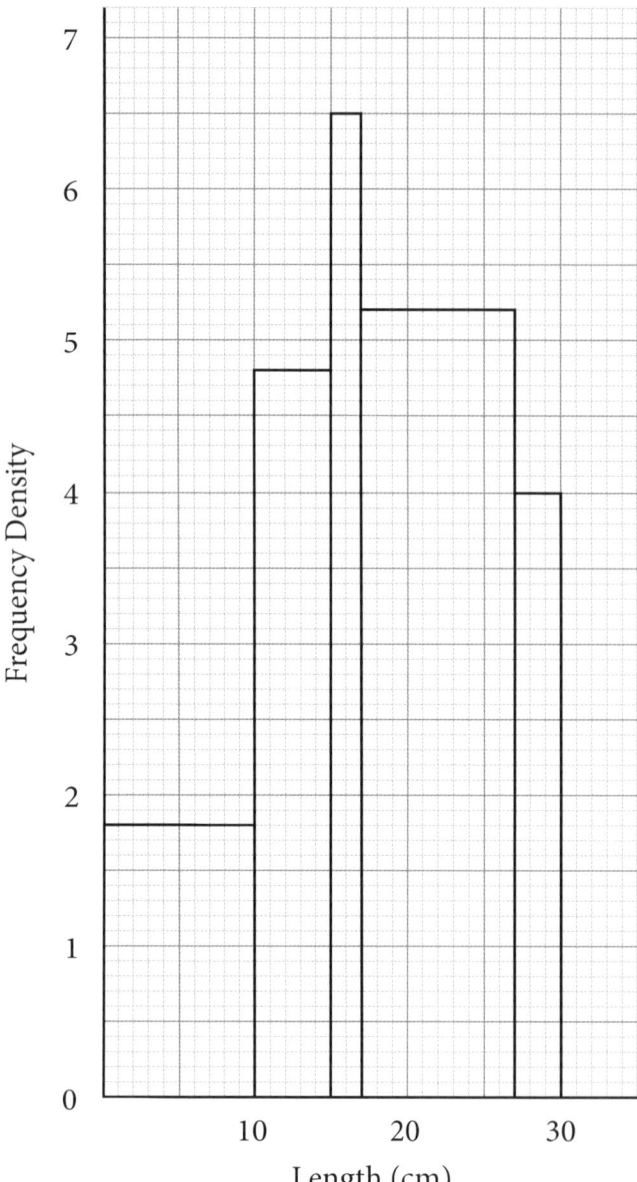

Work out:
(a) the mean length,

Answer _____

(b) the median length.

Answer _____

Revision Exercise 5

8. A solid consists of a cone base diameter 8.4 cm on top of a cube side 8.4 cm.
   The total height of the solid is 20 cm.
   Calculate:

   (a) the total volume of the solid,

   Answer _____

   (b) the total surface area of the solid.

   Answer _____

9. PQRS is a rhombus where P(–2, 1), Q(1, 3) and R(4, –7).
   Find:

   (a) the coordinates of the midpoint of PR,

   Answer _____

   (b) the equation of the line PR,

   Answer _____

   (c) the equation of the line QS.

   Answer _____

10. The curved surface area of a cylinder is 70 cm²
    The volume of the cylinder is 84 cm³
    Work out:

    (a) the radius,

    Answer _____

    (b) the height of the cylinder.

    Answer _____

11. Solve:
$4x(x + 2) = x(x - 2) + 8$

Answer _____

12. The table below shows the ages of people in a club.

Age (A years)	Frequency
$10 < A \leq 14$	16
$14 < A \leq 17$	26
$17 < A \leq 21$	18
$21 < A \leq 28$	24
$28 < A \leq 30$	31

A stratified sample of 36 people are selected at random from those people aged less than or equal to 21. How many in the sample are in the age range $13 < A \leq 17$.

Answer _____

13. The table below shows the widths of different objects.

Width (W cm)	Frequency
$4 < W \leq 10$	28
$10 < W \leq 18$	52
$18 < W \leq 25$	44
$25 < W \leq 40$	27
$40 < W \leq 50$	51

A stratified sample of 48 objects are selected at random from less than or equal to 30 cm. How many in the sample are less than or equal to 16 cm.

Answer _____

14. (a) Find the equation of the line which is perpendicular to $4y - 3x = 5$ and passes through $(1, -5)$.

Answer _____

(b) Find where this line intersects the line $y - x - 2 = 0$

Answer _____

Answers

Revision Exercise 1

1. (a) Large sq − small sq = $(4x \times 3x) - 2x(4x - 6)$
   = $12x^2 - 8x^2 + 12x = 4x^2 + 12x$ (b) $4x^2 + 12x = 40$;
   $x^2 + 3x - 10 = 0$; $(x + 5)(x - 2) = 0$; so $x = 2$ or -5;
   but the length can't be negative, so $x = 2$ cm
2. (a) Gradient = $4 \div 2 = 2$; using $y = mx + c$ gives:
   $y = 2x - 10$ (b) $y = 2x + 9$ (c) Gradient = $-\frac{1}{2}$ so:
   $y = -\frac{1}{2}x + 4$
3. (a) 86, 164, 204, 232 (b) points plotted, curve
   (c)(i) 14 (ii) $17.5 - 10 = 7.5$ (iii) $216 - 36 = 180$
   (d) 15% of 240 = 36, so discard above 204, height =
   20.5 cm (e) Box plot accurately drawn.
4. (a) $(4x - 3)(2n + c)$ (b) $(q - 8)(q + 5)$
   (c) $(f + 3)(-4f - 5)$ (d) $3(t - 4v)(t + 4v)$
5. (a) 0, $-\frac{1}{6}$ (b) 3, 6
6. $AB^2 = 37$, $BC^2 = 37$, $AC^2 = 74$ ∴ $AC^2 = AB^2 + BC^2$
   ; proof by Pythagoras' theorem. OR grad AB = 6,
   grad BC = $-\frac{1}{6}$, product = -1 ∴ ∠ABC is 90°
7. (a) 34° (b) 34° (c) 112° (d) 68°
8. 272, 216, 144, 344
   34, 27, 18, 43
9. (a) × each side by 4: $9 - 3x = 20 - 8x$; giving $x = \frac{11}{5}$
   (b) × each side by 12: $8x + 8 + 3x - 12 = 84$; giving
   $x = 8$ (c) × each side by 12: $(8x - 4) - (3x + 9) = 12$;
   giving $x = 5$
10. (a) $\frac{(m^2 - n^2)}{nm}$ (b) $\frac{(n^2 + 24)}{4n}$ (c) $\frac{11q}{4}$
11. (a) p = gradient = 3 (b) $q = y$ intercept = -6
12. (a) Square + triangle
    = $(2x + 6)(3x - 2) + \frac{1}{2}(2x)(2x + 6)$
    = $(6x^2 + 14x - 12) + (2x^2 + 6x) = 8x^2 + 20x - 12$
    (b) $8x^2 + 20x - 12 = 60$; so $2x^2 + 5x - 18 = 0$; so
    $(2x + 9)(x - 2) = 0$; giving $x = -4.5$ or 2; but length
    of a side can't be negative so $x = 2$
13. (a) $y = -4x + 2$ (b) $y = -4x + 8$ (c) $y = \frac{1}{4}x - 4$
14. (a) 56° (b) 62° (c) 28° (d) 152° (cyclic quadrilateral
    property)

Revision Exercise 2

1. (a) $-5, -2$ (b) $\frac{7}{4}, -\frac{7}{4}$ (c) $5, -8$
2. (a) $\frac{5}{2}, -\frac{5}{2}$ (b) $7, -5$ (c) $-\frac{4}{3}, 2$ (d) $-\frac{5}{2}, -\frac{2}{3}$ (e) $2, 4$
3. Frequency densities (found by dividing frequency
   by the size of each class): 38, 27, 34, 22, 14, 26
4. (a) $8x^2 - 22xy - 21y^2$ (b) $25a^2 - 60ab + 36b^2$
   (c) $-k^2 - 2km - 17m^2$
5. (a) $y = -\frac{4}{3}x + 8$ (b) $\frac{3}{4}$
6. (a) multiplying both sides by $x(x - 3)$ gives:
   $12(x - 3) + 6x = 4x(x - 3)$; so $4x^2 - 30x + 36 = 0$;
   $2x^2 - 15x + 18 = 0$; $(2x - 3)(x - 6)$; giving $x = 6$ or $\frac{3}{2}$
   (b) multiplying both sides by $x(x + 1)$ gives:
   $8(x + 1) - 3x = 3x(x + 1)$; so $3x^2 - 2x - 8 = 0$;
   $(3x + 4)(x - 2)$; giving $x = 2$ or $-\frac{4}{3}$
7. (a) Alternate segment theorem. (b) Opposite angles
   in a cyclic quadrilateral add up to 180°. (c) Angle
   between a tangent and a radius is 90°. (d) 104°
8. (a) $(20 \times 5.2) + (10 \times 3.7) + (30 \times 2.2) + (20 \times 4.8)$
   $+ (10 \times 2.8) = 331$ (b) Bar between 110 and 140 cm
   with frequency density 3.4
9. (a) $y = 4x + 2$ (b) $y = -\frac{1}{2}x + 2\frac{1}{2}$
10. multiplying both sides by $(2x - 1)(2 - x)$ gives:
    $5(2 - x) - 4(2x - 1) = 5(2x - 1)(2 - x)$;
    giving $10x^2 - 38x + 24 = 0$; so $5x^2 - 19x + 12 = 0$;
    $(5x - 4)(x - 3)$; giving $x = 3$ or $\frac{4}{5}$
11. (a) cos A = $2.8 \div 7$; giving A = 66.4°
    (b) tan 35 = EF $\div$ 8.2; giving EF = 5.74 cm
12. Least = $14.65 \times 7 = 102.55$ cm, greatest = 14.75×7
    = 103.25 cm
13. (a) Interest in 2nd year = $6056.96 - 5824 = 232.96$
    so $x = 4\%$ (b) $104\% = 5824$, so $1\% = 5824 \div 104$
    = 56; so $100\% = £5600$ (c) 4% of 6056.96 = 242.28
    so total = $6056.96 = 242.28$; so total
    = $6056.96 + 242.28 = £6299.24$
14. (a) Angle PSR = 90° + 40° so forming a right-angle
    triangle we have: cos 40 = QR $\div$ 9.4; giving QR =
    7.2 cm (b) Third side of the triangle = 6.0 cm (by
    Pythagoras' theorem); so PQ = 5.8 + 6.0 = 11.8 cm

Revision Exercise 3

1. (a) tan 28 = TP ÷ 1.26; giving TP = 0.67 m
   (b) PB = 0.54 m; tan B = 0.67 ÷ 0.54; so B = 51°
2. (a) 6.935 × 30 = 208.05 cm (b) minimum diameter
   = 2(3.235) = 6.47; 6.47 × 12 = 77.64 cm
3. (a) tan 58 = 24 ÷ XY; so XY = 15 m
   (b) 28.3 m (by Pythagoras' theorem)
4. (a) 56.5 × 8.75 = 494.375 (b) 55.5 ÷ 12.5 = 4.44
5. (a) 3 4 5 6 (b) The graph is a straight line and the equation of a straight line is $y = mx + c$
   (c)(i) 0.6 (gradient of graph) (ii) 7 (y intercept)
6. cos 54 = BD ÷ 9.6; giving BD = 5.64 cm;
   sin 42 = AB ÷ 5.64; giving AB = 3.77 cm
7. (a) 2.54, –0.788 (b) 0.198, –4.20
8. (a) multiplying both sides by 6 gives:
   $6 - 3x - (8x - 6) = 78$; giving $-11x = 66$; so $x = -6$
9. (a) multiplying both sides by $x(x - 3)$ gives:
   $18(x - 3) + 15x = 8x(x - 3)$; giving
   $18x - 54 + 15x = 8x^2 - 24x$; and hence
   $8x^2 - 57x + 54 = 0$ (b) $8x^2 - 57x + 54 = 0$ can be factorised to give $(8x - 9)(x - 6) = 0$; so $x = 6$ or $9/8$
10. (a) $5.25^2 = 27.5625$ (b) 8.45 ÷ 7.85 = 1.08
    (c) 7.85 – 5.35 = 2.5
11. (a) 58° (b) 116° (c) 32° (d) 64°
12. 4 years
13. (a)(i) $3a(a + 2)$ (ii) $\dfrac{3a(a + 2)}{(a - 2)(a + 2)} = \dfrac{3a}{a - 2}$
    (b)(i) $(x - 3)(x + 1)$ (ii) $\dfrac{(x - 3)(x + 1)}{(x - 3)(x - 2)} = \dfrac{x + 1}{x - 2}$
    (c)(i) $(t + 4)(t + 7)$ (ii) $\dfrac{(t + 4)(t + 7)}{(t + 7)(t - 2)} = \dfrac{t + 4}{t - 2}$
14. (a) 20 (b) From bottom: 40, 80, 120, 160

    (c)
9–12	13–17	18–20	21–30
192	540	84	1240

Revision Exercise 4

1. (a) $\dfrac{(x - 5)(x + 3)}{(x + 3)(x - 3)} = \dfrac{x - 5}{x - 3}$ (b) $\dfrac{(x - 7)(x - 3)}{(x - 3)(x + 2)} = \dfrac{x - 7}{x + 2}$
   (c) $\dfrac{(2x - 3)(x + 2)}{(2x - 3)(3x - 1)} = \dfrac{x + 2}{3x - 1}$
   (d) $\dfrac{(4x - 1)(4x + 1)}{3x(4x + 1)} = \dfrac{4x - 1}{3x}$
   (e) $\dfrac{(x - 2)(x + 1)}{(x - 5)(x - 2)} = \dfrac{x + 1}{x - 5}$ (f) $\dfrac{(x + 3)(x + 4)}{(x - 2)(x + 4)} = \dfrac{x + 3}{x - 2}$
2. (a) area of S = area of R, so:
   $(3x - 2)(3x - 2) = (x + 2)(7x - 10)$;
   $9x^2 - 12x + 4 = 7x^2 + 4x - 20$; $x^2 - 8x + 12 = 0$
   (b) $x^2 - 8x + 12 = 0$ can be factorised as:
   $(x - 6)(x - 2)$ giving $x = 2$ or 6
3. (a) $4(x + 2) + x + 5 = (x + 5)(x + 2)$; giving
   $x^2 + 2x - 3 = 0$; or $(x + 3)(x - 1) = 0$; so $x = 1$ or -3
   (b) $10(x - 2) - 2(x + 1) = (x + 1)(x - 2)$; giving
   $x^2 - 9x + 20 = 0$; or $(x - 5)(x - 4) = 0$; so $x = 4$ or 5
4. Area = π × 30 ÷ 360 = 9.424 cm²;
   pressure = force ÷ area = 56 ÷ 9.424 = 5.94 N/cm
5. (a) 21.5 (b) 9 (c) 27 (d) 18
6. 456 + 342 + 513 = 1311; 69 ÷ 1311 × 456 = 24
7. (a) 8.45 + 1.75 = 10.2 (b) least value of B – C
   = 9.65 – 5.35 = 4.3; 8.35 × 4.3 = 35.905
8. $\sqrt{7.45^2 + 6.85^2} = 10.12$ cm
9. (a) Quarter circle area = $¼πr^2$ = 28.27; triangle area = $½bh$ = 18; 28.27 – 18 = 10.27 cm
   (b) Curved length = $¼πd$ = 9.42; diagonal = 8.49 (by Pythagoras' theorem); 8.49 + 9.42 = 17.91 cm
10. Largest rect = 8.45 × 3.25 = 27.46; smallest circle
    = $πr^2$ = π × 1.35^2 = 5.72; 27.46 – 5.72 = 21.74 cm²
11. (a) $\sqrt{16.5^2 - 11.5^2} = 11.83$ cm
    (b) 44.18°
12. (a) $\dfrac{10x - 2}{(x - 3)(2x + 1)}$ (b) $\dfrac{-x + 29}{(3x - 2)(x + 5)}$
13. $\dfrac{20}{(x + 3)} + \dfrac{36}{(2x - 1)} = \dfrac{76x + 88}{(x + 3)(2x - 1)}$ hours
14. (a) Venn diagram with sets A, B, C: 7 in A only; 5 in A∩B; 9 in B only; 4 in A∩B∩C; 2 in A∩C; 6 in B∩C; 8 in C only; 11 outside (b) 11

Answers

Revision Exercise 5

1. (a) Hemisphere vol = ½ × 4/3πr^3 = 56.55 cm³;
   cylinder vol = πr^2h = 339.29 cm³; total = 395.84 cm³
   (b) Hemisphere area = ½ × 4πr^2 = 56.54 cm²;
   cylinder area = 2πrh = 226.19; total = 282.73 cm²

2. Full cone height: tan 75 = h_f ÷ 6; h_f = 22.39; top cone height: tan 75 = h_t ÷ 1.5; h_t = 5.60; vol full cone − vol top cone = (π$r^2 h_f$ ÷ 3) − (π$r^2 h_t$ ÷ 3) = 830.89 cm³

3. Full cone height = 22.51 (by Pythagoras' theorem); slanted height of top cone = 22.86 − 16 = 6.86; height of top cone = 6.75 (by Pythagoras' theorem); vol full cone − vol top cone = (πr^2 × 22.51 ÷ 3) − (πr^2 × 6.75 ÷ 3) = 367 cm³ (to nearest cm²)

4. Slanted height of full cone = 14.6 (by Pythagoras' theorem); slanted height of top cone = 4.9 (by Pythagoras' theorem); curved surface area = (π × 2.4 × 14.6) − (π × 0.8 × 4.9) = 98 cm³ (to nearest cm²)

5. (a)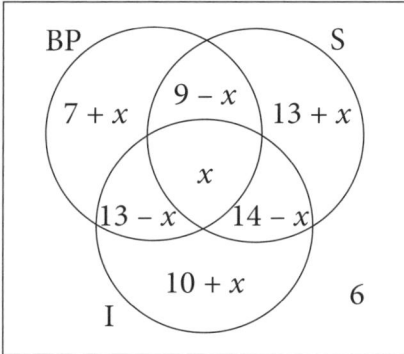

   (b) 5 (c) 21

6. Total number of objects = 125; total weight of all objects = 3377.5; 3377.5 ÷ 125 = 27.02 kg

7. (a) Total number of objects = 119; total length of all objects = 2084; 2084 ÷ 119 = 17.51 cm
   (b) median = 59th item; this is in the 4th class, objects 55–107, a total of 52 objects; as it is the 5th item in this class, 5 ÷ 52 = 0.096 × 10 cm [range of this class] = 0.96; 0.96 + 17 [lower bound of this class] = 17.96 cm

8. (a) Cone vol + cube vol = 214.28 + 592.70 = 806.99 cm (b) SA cone = 62.82; SA cube = 423.36; area of base of cone [which is not visible] = 55.42; 162.82 + 423.36 − 55.42 = 530.76 cm

9. (a) (1, −3) (b) $y = -\frac{4}{3}x - \frac{5}{3}$
   (c) $y = \frac{3}{4}x - 3\frac{3}{4}$ or $y = \frac{3}{4}x - \frac{15}{4}$

10. (a) Volume: 84 = πr^2h; area: 70 = 2πrh; dividing 1st equation by 2nd gives: 1.2 = ½r, so r = 2.4 cm
    (b) 70 = 2π × 2.4h; so h = 4.64 cm

11. $4x^2 + 8x = x^2 - 2x + 8$; giving $3x^2 + 10x - 8 = 0$; $(3x - 2)(x + 4)$ giving $x = \frac{2}{3}$ or −4

12. 18

13. 24 or 25

14. (a) $4y = 3x + 5$ can be rearranged as $y = \frac{3}{4}x + \frac{5}{4}$; so $m = \frac{3}{4}$; then using $y = mx + c$ gives: $y + 5 = -\frac{4}{3}(x - 1)$; $y = -\frac{4}{3}x - \frac{11}{3}$
    (b) $y - x - 2 = 0$ can be rearranged as $y = x + 2$; so at the point of intersection: $x + 2 = -\frac{4}{3}x - \frac{11}{3}$; giving $x = -\frac{17}{7}$; substituting x back gives $y = -\frac{3}{7}$; so solution = $(-\frac{17}{7}, -\frac{3}{7})$

Meeting the requirements of the two-tier CCEA GCSE Mathematics specification, this is one of eight revision booklets to cover levels M1 to M8. These valuable questions were specially commissioned for the booklet and are not from past papers. Full answers are included at the rear and contain not only the final answer but, where appropriate, an indication of the process required to reach the given solution. The book has been through a meticulous quality assurance process by a GCSE Mathematics expert.

Which revision booklets do I need?

Students sitting CCEA GCSE Mathematics will usually be in one of four pathways and will require two revision booklets. The student's teacher will be able to advise which pathway they are studying.

If the student is studying this pathway...	...they will need these revision booklets
Foundation Tier Option 1	M1 and M5
Foundation Tier Option 2	M2 and M6
Higher Tier Option 1	M3 and M7
Higher Tier Option 2	M4 and M8

COLOURPOINT EDUCATIONAL

ISBN 978-1-78073-195-7

www.colourpoint.co.uk